MAP OF JAMAICA

showing approximate location of places discussed in the text; such places are printed in italic type, thus: *Lucea*.

Note: a number of the places described (Rockfort, Hope Gardens, Bellevue, etc.) are close to Kingston and are not specially named on the map.

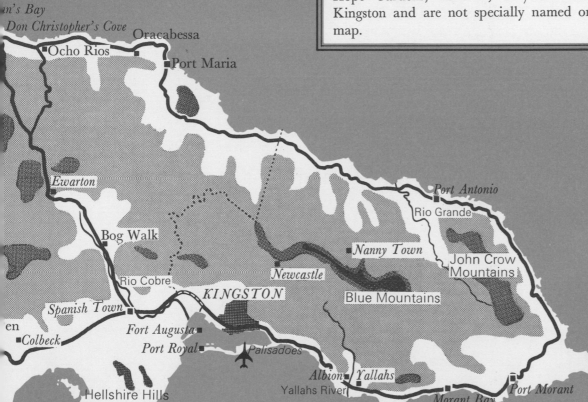

an's Bay
Don Christopher's Cove Oracabessa
Ocho Rios Port Maria

Ewarton

Bog Walk

Port Antonio
Rio Grande

Nanny Town John Crow Mountains

Rio Cobre *Newcastle*

KINGSTON Blue Mountains

Spanish Town

en *Colbeck* *Fort Augusta* Port Royal *Palisadoes*

Hellshire Hills *Albion* *Yallahs*
Yallahs River Morant Bay *Port Morant*

S E A

HISTORIC
Jamaica
FROM THE AIR

Photographs by Jack Tyndale-Biscoe

Text by David Buisseret

for Hae. still searching for the enigma within the conundrum!   David Buisseret   Vancouver 1992

CARIBBEAN UNIVERSITIES PRESS

PREFACE

Having worked a certain amount in Europe on historical studies involving aerial photography, I was naturally eager to use this technique in Jamaica. At first my wife and I tried to take our own photographs, but these were so inadequate beside the ones Jack Tyndale-Biscoe was publishing in the *Gleaner* that we decided to ask him if he would care to undertake a collaborative work.

The present book is the result of that collaboration, which has now extended over two or three years. In some cases aerial photographs existed, for which it was then necessary to find matching plans and commentaries; in rather more cases the aerial photographs were specially taken to fit the old plans, drawn from a wide variety of sources. We are most grateful to the British Museum, to the Hispanic Society of America, to the Institute of Jamaica, to the Jamaica Archives and to the Public Record Office (London) for supplying us with material.

The plan on which the plates are presented is a historical one, since that seemed the best way to bring out their significance. We realise, of course, that we ha omitted many promising subjects, and that there may be errors in the commentary; that is almost inevitable in a compilation of this type, in spite of the kindness of Clinton Black, who read the manuscript for us.

We hope, all the same, that this little book will prov useful, not only for visitors who want to explore and understand Jamaica, but also for Jamaicans, who may enjoy seeing their island from an unaccustomed angle.

David Buisseret   Mona 18 April 19

106908

FIRST PUBLISHED 1969 BY

CARIBBEAN UNIVERSITIES PRESS LTD BARBADOS

© 1969 DAVID BUISSERET & JACK TYNDALE-BISCOE

DESIGNED BY CECIL BOURCHIER MSIA

PRINTED IN ENGLAND BY FLETCHER & CO LTD NORWICH

SBN 602 21322 3

ONTENTS

The British Period: 1865 and 1907

Independent Jamaica

HISTORICAL INTRODUCTION

The history of all countries is to some degree determined by their geography, and this has been particularly true of Jamaica. The island consists essentially of a hilly spine, fringed by coastal plains formed by the great rivers. The plains often form rich agricultural land, and although much of the mountainous area is not very fertile, here and there in the hills are pockets of land which can bear abundantly.

The indigenous people were called Arawaks, but little of their primitive culture survives, except for a few place-names (the Museum of White Marl, on the Spanish Town road, has a permanent exhibit of these relics). When the Spaniards colonised the island in the early sixteenth century, this peaceful people rapidly died out, unaccustomed as they were either to work or to European diseases like smallpox. So the Spaniards were soon in undisputed control of Jamaica, which was useful to them chiefly as a replenishing-place for the great galleons homeward bound from the Spanish Main. With so many rich possessions on the other islands and the mainland, the Spaniards hardly needed to exploit Jamaica's resources; she produced some hides and lard, but the population remained scanty and even in the mid-seventeenth century reached only about 6,000, of whom half were slaves.

By then, of course, the Spaniards were having to defend their scattered possessions in the New World against the greed of the other European powers. The English had raided Jamaica in 1596, and again in 1603, 1640 and 1643; in 1655 they sent to the Caribbean a fleet of 38 ships and about 8,000 men, which after an abortive attempt on Santo Domingo turned on Jamaica. The Spaniards were evidently incapable of resisting an assault by so large a force, and most of them retired to Cuba, though a handful of brave men under Don Cristobal Isassi maintained a guerilla resistance until 1660.

The English were quick to see the economic potential of their new possession, with its fertile plains. At first its prosperity was based mainly on the buccaneering expeditions which went out from Port Royal, but after 1680 exports of agricultural produce began to increase fast, with sugar rapidly coming to the fore as the main crop. Large numbers of African slaves were imported to work the plantations, and great fortunes were made in the sugar business. Needless to say, this prosperity attracted the jealousy of the other European powers, and eventually of the infant United States of America; it was against these potential invaders that the fortresses illustrated in this book were constructed.

By the early nineteenth century the whole system of producing sugar with slave labour was coming under severe criticism in England, for both economic and humanitarian reasons, and in 1834 the Emancipation Act was passed. In Jamaica many of the freed slaves left the plantations, and established themselves in remote settlements in the hills, but the coming of personal freedom did not necessarily mean an improvement in their material condition. Indeed, in some cases they may have been economically worse off than before, and to this hardship was added the scandalous inadequacy of the judicial services.

These conditions led to a smouldering discontent which was fanned into open fire in 1865, when the Morant Bay rebellion broke out against Governor Eyre's repressions and injustices. The revolt was of course crushed, and a disproportionate repression ensued. However, the very excesses of this retaliation were in a sense productive, in that Governor Eyre was recalled and the island was more closely linked to Great Britain as a Crown Colony. Governors came out with wider powers, and were able to push through far-reaching reforms in the judicial and administrative structures.

Slowly a new Jamaica began to take shape, based on the new constitutional structure; there was a certain recovery in the sugar industry, and in spite of the disastrous earthquake of 1907 the island seemed to be making progress. With this progress, however, came increasing discontent at the tutelage of Great Britain. This discontent became sharper in the 1930s, when the suffering brought on by the world-wide economic depression led to outbreaks of violence, particularly at Frome (Westmoreland) in 1938. From these disorders emerged the commanding figure of Alexander Bustamante, who with his cousin and political rival Norman Manley led Jamaica during the decades preceding independence in 1962.

The coming of independence found Jamaica facing grave economic and social problems. The sugar and banana industries each had serious weaknesses, and the flight from the countryside was putting intolerable pressure on facilities of every kind in Kingston. On the other hand, the bauxite and tourist industries were flourishing, and full of promise for the future; the island had at least a good chance of significantly raising the standard of life of her people.

BIBLIOGRAPHY

For a historical introduction to the island, there is C. V. Black's *History of Jamaica* (London 1961). Frank Cundall's *Historic Jamaica* (London 1915, long out of print) remains an excellent guide, especially to Kingston and the surrounding areas; it may now be supplemented by Philip Wright and Paul White's *Exploring Jamaica* (London 1969), which is in general strong where Cundall was weak, geographically speaking. The Jamaica Information Service publishes an interesting series of pamphlets called *Facts on Jamaica*, and there is a good general survey by Barry Floyd in *Focus on Jamaica*, one of the occasional publications of the American Geographical Society. On more particular points, there are often useful articles in the *Jamaican Historical Review* and in the *Bulletin* (mimeographed) of the Jamaican Historical Society, as well as in *The Daily Gleaner*.

The following books and articles contain material relating to the subjects covered in this book. They are listed in the order in which the relevant subjects appear in the book.

Cotter, C. S., 'The Discovery of the Spanish carvings at Seville'
    Jamaican Historical Review, i no 3(1948) 227–233

ñiguez, D. Angulo, *El gótico y el renacimento en las Antillas*
    (Seville 1947)

Jacobs, H. P., 'The Spanish period of Jamaican history'
    Jamaican Historical Review, iii no 1(1957) 79–93

Padron, F. Morales, *Jamaica española* (Seville 1952)

Black, C. V., *Spanish Town* (Spanish Town 1960)

Cotter, C. S., 'Don Christopher's Cove'
    Jamaican Historical Review, ii no 3(1953) 39–43

Bryce, W., *Historic Port Royal* (Kingston 1952)

Young, J. G., 'Who planned Kingston?'
    Jamaican Historical Review, i no 2(1946) 144–153

Buisseret, D. J., 'The Fortifications of Kingston-Port Royal,
    1655–1815' *Bulletin*, iv (1968) 288

Buisseret, D. J., *art. cit.* iv (1967) 216–218

Feulon, A. E., 'The Windward Maroons'
    Bulletin, iv (1968) 304–9

Buisseret, D. J., 'The Fortifications of Kingston-Port Royal,
    1655–1815' *Bulletin*, iv (1968) 309–10

Mulloch, G., *Newcastle* (mimeographed, Newcastle 1965)

Craton, M., & Walvin, J., are preparing for publication a history of
    Worthy Park—on which there is no work currently available

Cundall, F., 'An Historic Jamaica Estate'
    West India Committee Circular xlii (1927) 369 *et seq.*

Cole, M., 'Useful Great House'
    The Sunday Gleaner, 30 May 1965

Buisseret, D. J., 'Who did build Colbeck Castle?'
    Bulletin, iv (1966) 159–60

Concannon, T. A. L., 'Colbeck Castle'
    Bulletin, iv (1966) 88–94

Jacobs, H. P., 'The Colbeck Papers'
    Jamaican Historical Review, iii no 3(1962) 39–67

Fremmer, R., 'Fulford Great House'
    The Daily Gleaner 2 December 1964

du Quesnay, F. J., 'Rose Hall Great House'
    The Daily Gleaner 4 April 1964

Robertson, G., 'The Rose Hall legend'
    Jamaica Journal ii no 4 (1968) 6–12

Shore, J., *In Old St James* (London 1952)

Olivier, Sir Sydney, *The myth of Governor Eyre* (London 1933)

Semmel, B., *Jamaican blood and Victorian conscience* (Boston 1963)

Black, C. V., 'Hospitality under Eyre' *Bulletin*, ii (1958) 106–108

Casserly, F. L., 'A Great Sea-raider's links with Jamaica'
    Bulletin, ii (1958) 108–112

Sibley, I., 'Flamstead in the Port Royal mountains'
    The Sunday Gleaner 4 December 1960

Anon: article in *The Daily Gleaner* 23 April 1934

The Spanish Period:

Plate 1 reproduces a map of the early seventeenth century by Gerard Mercator, to show the site of Seville (Seviglia), the first Spanish settlement, founded in 1510. In the past few decades much work has been done at this site, mostly by Mr C. S. Cotter, working under the auspices of the Institute of Jamaica.

In the aerial photograph and the accompanying sketch this excavation-work stands out around the fort, in the coconut grove. On the hill above the grove stands Seville great house, which may one day become the main museum in Jamaica for monuments of the Spanish period; a little way to the east may be seen the Columbus monument, by the entrance-drive to the Catholic church. Alas, this modern structure was built partly by destroying the old Spanish church, whose remains may still be seen a little to the west of the present church.

The reef off St Ann's Bay is very clear in the aerial photograph, as also is the entrance-channel through it. Somewhere within this sheltered area probably lie the remains of the ships beached by Columbus in 1503, when the great mariner was marooned for a little more than a year in Jamaica.

The settlement at Seville was not a prosperous one; the Spaniards' children seemed especially vulnerable to disease there, and so about 1524 they moved their capital to a site on the southern plains (Villa de la Vega; see below, under 'Spanish Town').

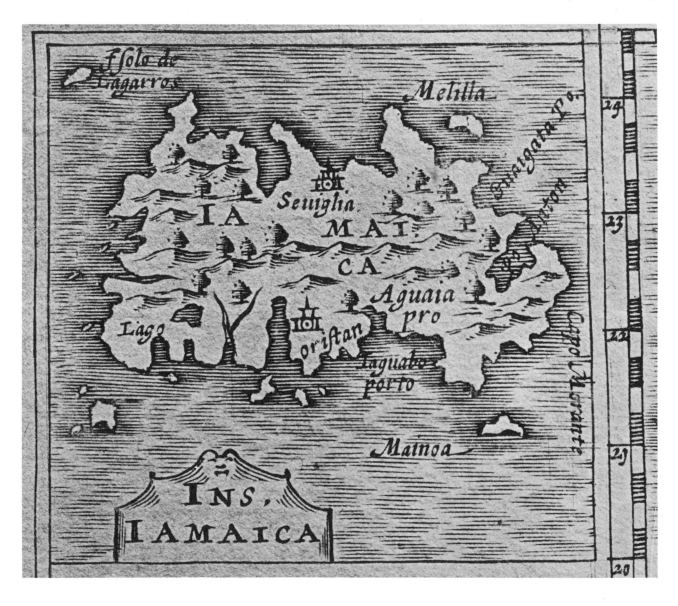

2

The First Settlement

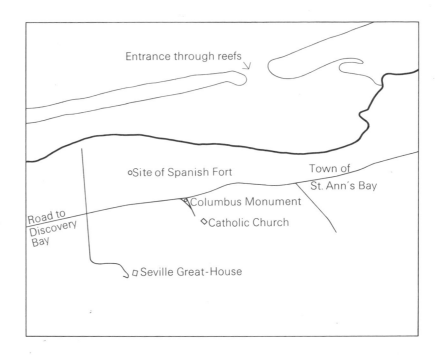

Entrance through reefs

Site of Spanish Fort

Town of
St. Ann's Bay

Columbus Monument

Road to
Discovery
Bay

Catholic Church

Seville Great-House

tail from a map by Gerard Mercator (1609)
show the site of Seville

rial view of Seville and St Ann's Bay

The Spanish Period:

The site which the Spaniards chose for their new capital was on the western bank of the Rio Cobre, a little way south of the gorge (see pages 6–7). There they laid out a new town in the fashion common in the New World, an irregular chequer-board. At the height of its prosperity under the Spaniards this town, *Saint Jago de la Vega*, had four or five hundred houses, five or six well-built churches, and a Franciscan monastery.

Today evidence of this Spanish period has almost entirely disappeared. To the north of the great square (1) there are, it is true, Monk Street, Red Church Street and White Church Street, and the general plan of the town reflects its origin. But the rambling palace on the central square was pulled down in the eighteenth century to make way for the English governor's house, and the Anglican cathedral has long obscured the remains of the main Spanish church.

In their turn, the street-names of 1767 have moved with later fashion. Broad Street has become King Street, Western Street is now Nugent Street (after Lady Nugent's husband), and Jew Street has become Old Market Street; the present market is in fact near the site of the Negroe Market. Although the last two centuries have not treated it well, Spanish Town retains some of the distinction of its past, and may well enjoy a more prosperous future, as industrial enterprises are established there.

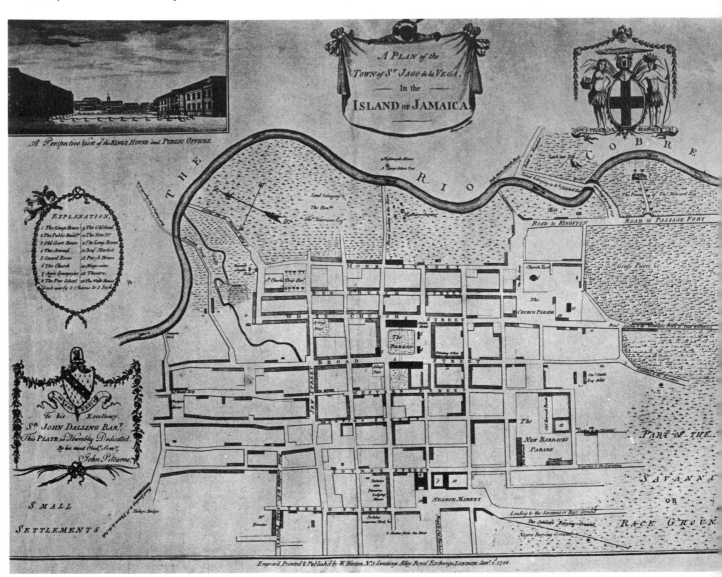

Spanish Town

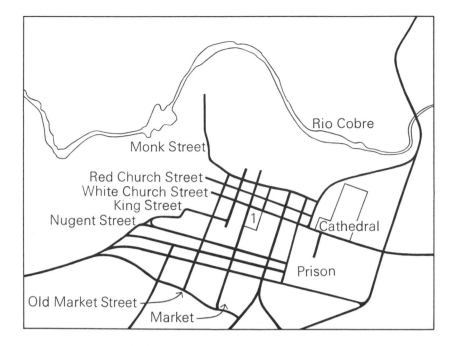

...an of 1786 by John Pitcarne of Spanish Town

...rial view of Spanish Town

The Spanish Period:

The Gorge of the Rio Cobre

he site of Spanish Town had the
rategic advantage of controlling
e southern exit from the gorge of
e Rio Cobre. On page 6 may be
en the sinuous course of the Rio
obre, winding its way under high
uffs between Bog Walk and
panish Town. The road follows the
ver, first on one bank and then,
ter Flat Bridge, on the other.
he Spaniards are said to have
tablished a small fort just north of
at Bridge, and with this they
ould have been able to command
e defile.

On either side of the Rio Cobre
e the precipitous broken hills so
aracteristic of central Jamaica.
ven now there are few routes in
is area, and the roads which do
ist are often forced, as is clear from
e aerial photograph, to meander
a halt.

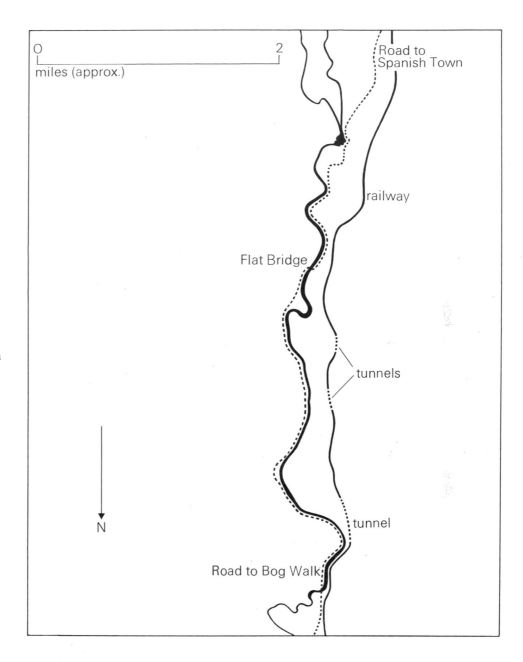

ial view of the Rio Cobre between Bog Walk
Spanish Town

The Spanish Period: *A Ranch*

The aerial photograph shows the lower Yallahs valley, part of the former *hato*, or pasture, of Ayala. This valley is typical of those through which the Jamaican rivers reach the sea, and it is easy to imagine that the Spaniards found this good ranching country.

Notice from the aerial photograph how closely the hills hem in the plain, and how vulnerable the ford looks on the Kingston-Morant Bay road. Notice too how the roads penetrate the hills, but then come to an abrupt halt.

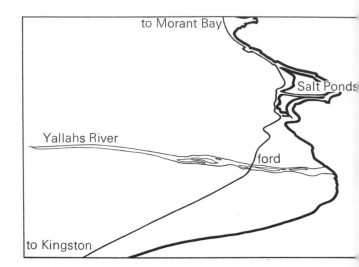

The Departure of the Spaniards

used to be thought that the ...aniards evacuated Jamaica ...thout much resistance, after the ...ding of the English in what is now ...ngston harbour in 1655. However, ...ce the publication of S.A.G. ...ylor's *The Western design* in 1965 it ...s become clear that during five ...ars there was bitter guerilla ...rfare, in which the Spaniards ...l out in the hills, making ...riodical forays to pick off imprudent English soldiers.

The leader of these Spanish guerillas was a certain Don Cristobal Isassi, and his constant aim was to get help from Spain so as to establish a strong headquarters on the north side of the island. In May 1658 he did receive reinforcements, and began to fortify a point near the mouth of the Rio Nuevo. However, word of his doings reached the English commander-in-chief, Edward d'Oyley, who sailed round from Port Royal and after a bitter struggle put the Spaniards to flight. Isassi fought on for another two years, but was eventually forced to retreat to Cuba; it is possible that he set sail from this Don Christopher's Cove in St Ann, though there is another Don Christopher's Cove in St Mary with equally strong claims.

The British Period:

The Spaniards had not settled at what is now Port Royal, for they used Old Harbour as the port of access to Spanish Town. When the English had secured the island, however, they rapidly saw to the fortification of the western tip of the long peninsula which nearly encloses Kingston harbour.

After 1655 the town of Port Royal grew apace, at first as a base for the buccaneers, and later as the main English centre for Caribbean trade. By 1690 it probably had about 2,000 houses, half of which were substantial brick structures, and a population of about 8,000, including many wealthy merchants and one or two good doctors. It is false to imagine Port Royal of the 1680s merely as a rough and ready seaport, for life there was by then at least as stable, luxurious and well-organized as in most contemporary European towns of similar size.

All that, of course, came to an en[d] in the earthquake of 1692. The plan of 1782 clearly shows the 'part sunk by the earthquake', to the north-we[st] of the peninsula; this catastrophe was followed in 1703 by a fire, and i[n] 1712 and 1722 by disastrous hurricanes, after which the commercial primacy shifted definitively to Kingston, though Po[rt] Royal remained a great naval cent[re]

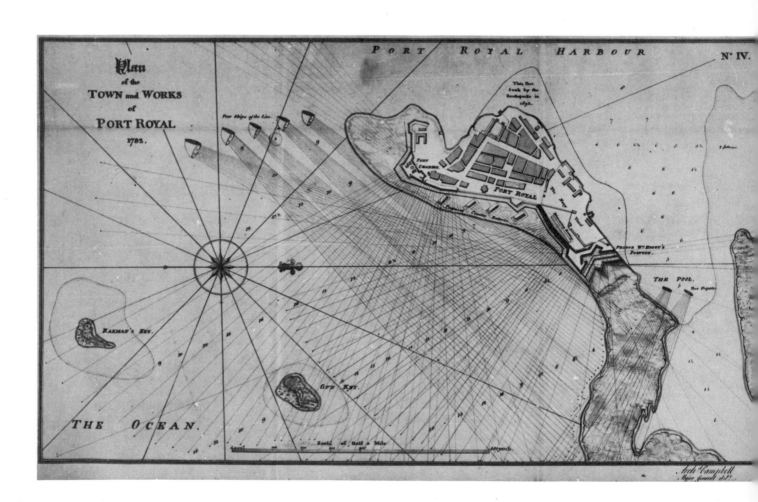

Plan of Port Royal in 1782, drawn by Major-General Campbell

Aerial photograph of Port Royal

Early Towns

On the aerial photograph Fort Charles is clearly recognizable, as is the outline of the northern bastion of Prince William Henry's Polygon (Battery); there are also several other interesting features, like the four massive gun-pits dug during the reign of Queen Victoria, and the early nineteenth-century naval hospital, which is now the centre for archeological research at Port Royal.

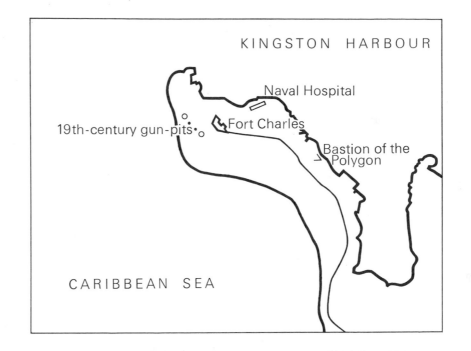

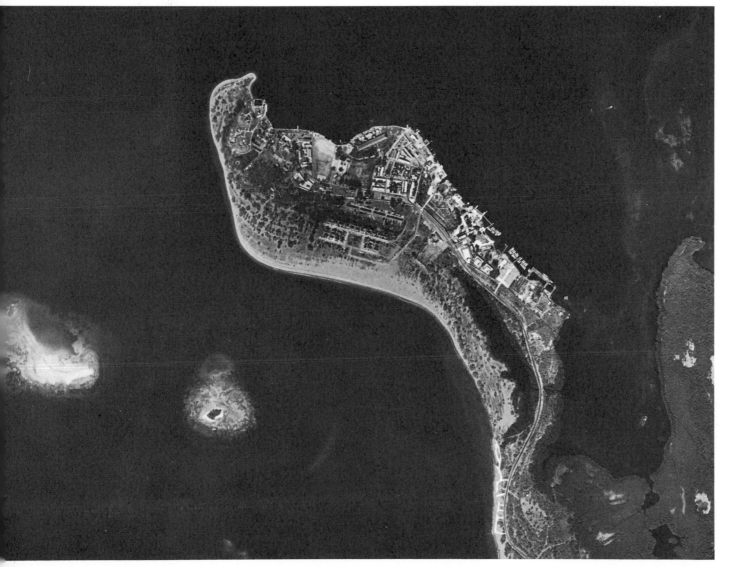

The British Period:

Even a cursory glance at these two plates shows how closely the heart of Kingston still conforms to the early eighteenth-century plan. Most of the street-names have remained the same, except that Peck, Bernard, Burden, White (Blanche), Morden, Black Marsh and Sutton have given way to the streets of which they were formerly extensions (e.g. Bernard Street has now become part of Beeston Street).

Nothing now remains of the 'magazines' in the north-western corner of Victoria Park, or indeed of the well in its centre, but the site of the Kingston Parish Church is clearly identifiable. From the aerial photograph it is easy to see how the symmetry of the ancient plan has slowly been lost, with the diagonal intrusion of the railway to the north-west, and the irregular streets around Kingston College to the north-east.

This early plan of Kingston was probably drawn up not, as the caption on the engraving says, by Colonel Christian Lilly, but by a certain John Goffe, after the earthquake of 1692 which destroyed a large part of Port Royal.

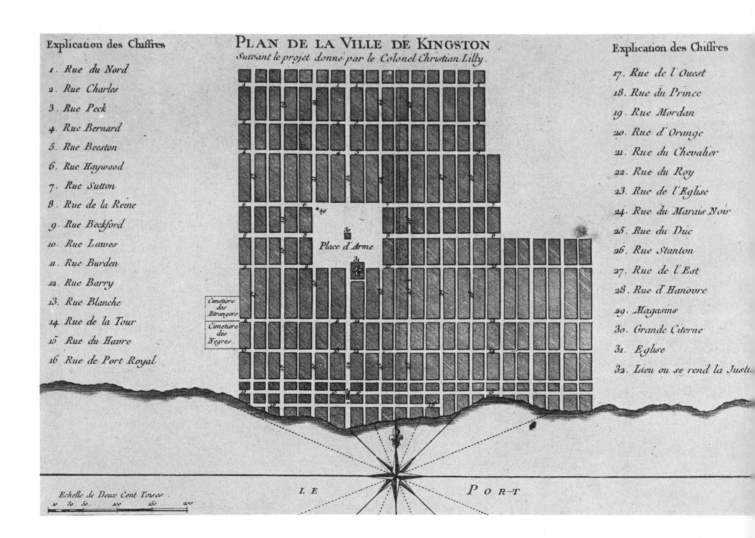

PLAN DE LA VILLE DE KINGSTON
Suivant le projet donné par le Colonel Christian Lilly.

Explication des Chiffres

1. Rue du Nord
2. Rue Charles
3. Rue Peck
4. Rue Bernard
5. Rue Beeston
6. Rue Haywood
7. Rue Sutton
8. Rue de la Reine
9. Rue Beckford
10. Rue Lawes
11. Rue Burden
12. Rue Barry
13. Rue Blanche
14. Rue de la Tour
15. Rue du Havre
16. Rue de Port Royal

Explication des Chiffres

17. Rue de l'Ouest
18. Rue du Prince
19. Rue Mordan
20. Rue d'Orange
21. Rue du Chevalier
22. Rue du Roy
23. Rue de l'Eglise
24. Rue du Marais Noir
25. Rue du Duc
26. Rue Stanton
27. Rue de l'Est
28. Rue d'Hanovre
29. Magasins
30. Grande Citerne
31. Eglise
32. Lieu ou se rend la Justi.

Place d'Arme

Cimetière des Etrangers
Cimetière des Negres

Echelle de Deux Cent Toises.

LE PORT

Plan of Kingston by J.-B. Bellin (17

Early Towns

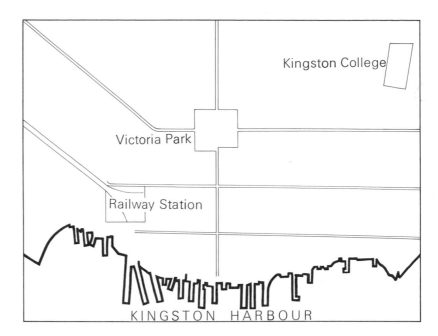

...rial view of downtown Kingston

The British Period:

During his first visit to Jamaica in 1494, Columbus anchored briefly in Montego Bay. The town did not, however, attain great importance until the later eighteenth century, when it became one of the centres for the export of sugar; it is now, of course, a major tourist centre and has about 30,000 inhabitants.

The old town was several times destroyed by fire, and so it is rather surprising that the plan of 1765 conforms so closely to the modern layout. Most of the streets mentioned on the plan are still recognizable, though George Street has disappeared, and Harbour Street has grown up beyond Strand Street

on the seaward side. Where the creek formerly was, is now Creek Street; Barnett Street remains unchanged.

On the aerial photograph may be seen not only the extensive suburban development around the town, but also the closely-packed shacks of the North Gully—a striking contrast.

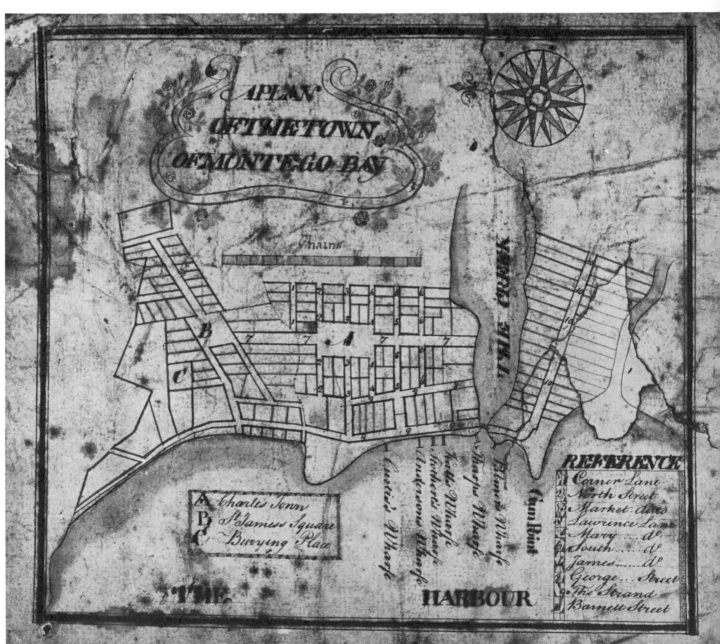

14

Early Towns

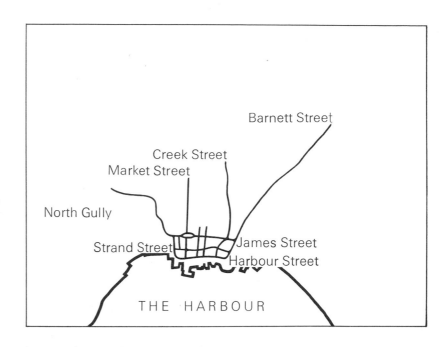

Barnett Street

Creek Street

Market Street

North Gully

Strand Street

James Street

Harbour Street

THE HARBOUR

*Plan of Montego Bay about 1765 by
Samuel Vaughan (?)*

Aerial view of Montego Bay

The British Period:

Rockfort, where the Long Mountain comes down almost sheer into the harbour, was the natural point at which to block the eastern approaches to Kingston, and some kind of fortification was put up there as early as 1694. The present fort probably dates from 1729, and until quite recently the main road into Kingston ran through its impressive gateway.

The only original building now standing is the magazine, just to the left (west) of the 'captain's house'; the latter has been destroyed, but its foundations are visible just to the north of the present house. Also visible are the foundations of the 'soldiers' kitchen and storehouses' and of the 'barrack for 200 men', the former as a mark in the turf just north of the 'welcome' sign, and the latter as a turf-mark across the centre of the decorative lozenge. Rockfort's walls were once washed by the water of the harbour, but the aerial photograph shows that much land is now being reclaimed there.

Plan of Rockfort by Major McKerras, 1786

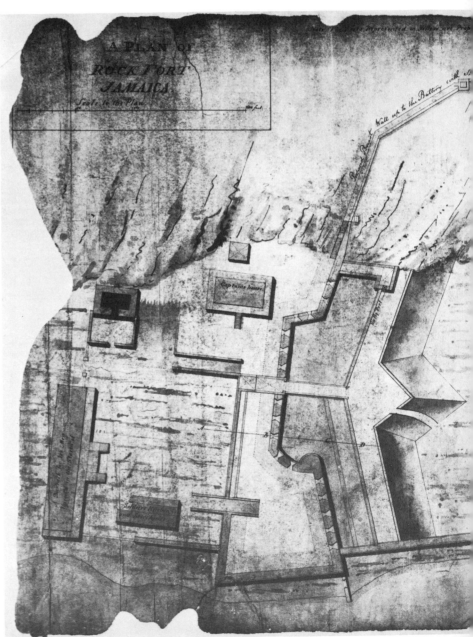

Fortifications

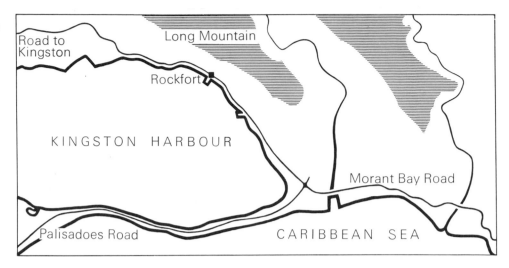

aerial view of Rockfort

The British Period:

When Kingston began to grow, in the early eighteenth century, it became apparent that the entrance to the inner bay needed to be defended, and in 1740 work was begun on the very difficult site at Mosquito Point. This stinking, muddy spit could only take heavy fortifications after long palmetto logs had been sunk deep into its subsoil; all the same, by 1755 a large fort had been constructed there, housing 80 heavy guns.

The main features of this structure are clearly visible today; indeed, the aerial photograph is amazingly faithful to the plan of 1782, even down to the details of buildings which have been razed (centre, left). Now, as then, Fort Augusta commands the ship channel, which runs to the south of the buoy, visible in the bottom right-hand corner of the aerial photograph. The old fort is now a prison, which may be visited on application to the Superintendent at the General Penitentiary.

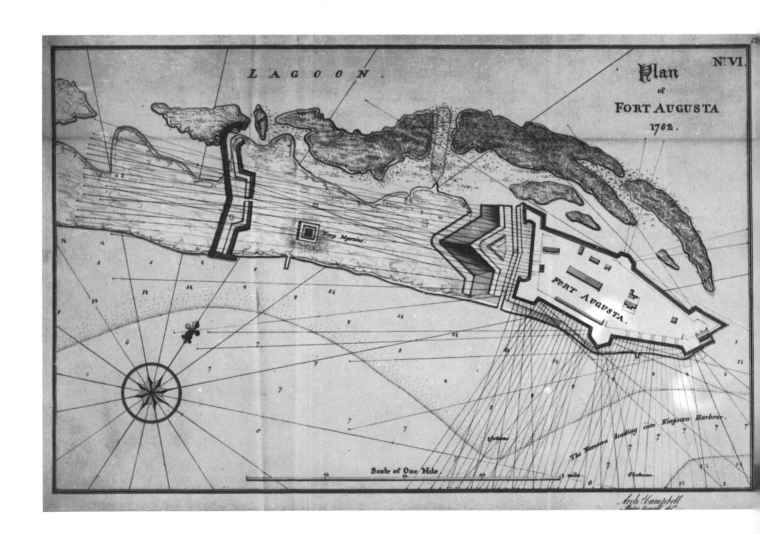

Plan of Fort Augusta in 1782, drawn by Major-General Campbell

Aerial view of Fort Augusta

Fortifications

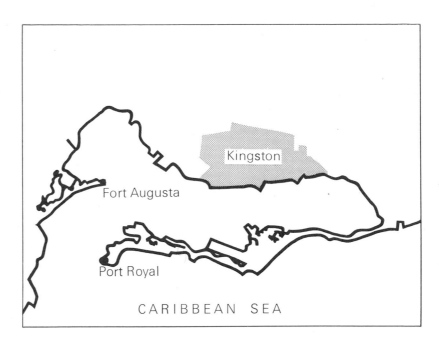

Kingston

Fort Augusta

Port Royal

CARIBBEAN SEA

The British Period:

Fortifications

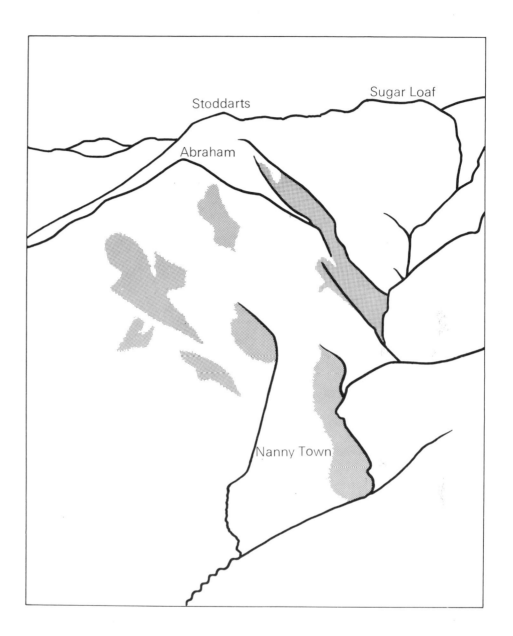

When the Spaniards were expelled, they freed many of their slaves, who fled to the mountains as Maroons (from the Spanish *cimarron*, a wild man). In time, as other slaves escaped, two leading Maroon kingdoms developed, one in the west-central area of the island, the cockpit country, and the other in the east, on the northern slopes of the Grand Ridge of the Blue Mountains. From these retreats the Maroons would emerge at night, setting fire to the settlers' crops, stealing their goods and slaughtering their cattle.

Attempts to crush them nearly always failed, whether conducted by regular soldiers or by settlers, for the Maroons were skilful woodsmen and excellent marksmen. In December 1734, however, an expedition commanded by a certain Colonel George Brooks succeeded in crossing the Blue Mountains from the south, and in attacking the Maroon settlement of Nanny Town, which then contained about 500 persons. Using the swivel-guns of Captain William Stoddart, the party succeeded in driving the Maroons from the town, and in occupying it. In July 1967 an expedition led by Ian Teulon of the Survey Department visited this site, and shortly afterwards a tablet was found on which were inscribed these words:

Decemb. 17. 1734
This town was took by col. Brook
And after kept by capt. Cooke
Till July 1735.

With the departure of Colonel Brook's expedition, the Maroons reoccupied their town; a little afterwards, in 1739, they were granted independent status, and ceased to be a menace.

Aerial view of the site of Nanny Town

The British Period:

It is clear from the aerial photograph how the chief town of Westmoreland got its name of 'plain by the sea'. Until recently its main street, Great George Street, was hemmed in by mangrove swamps, but these are now being cleared, as the photograph shows.

At the end of Great George Street there still stands the delightful little fort constructed about the middle of the eighteenth century. Inside the gate may still be seen the 'powder magazine' marked on the plan, and the general shape of the walls is quite recognizable, though the south-western section has fallen away. The 'stone causeway' has been built up, and to the west of it is now solid ground on which stand a sugar warehouse.

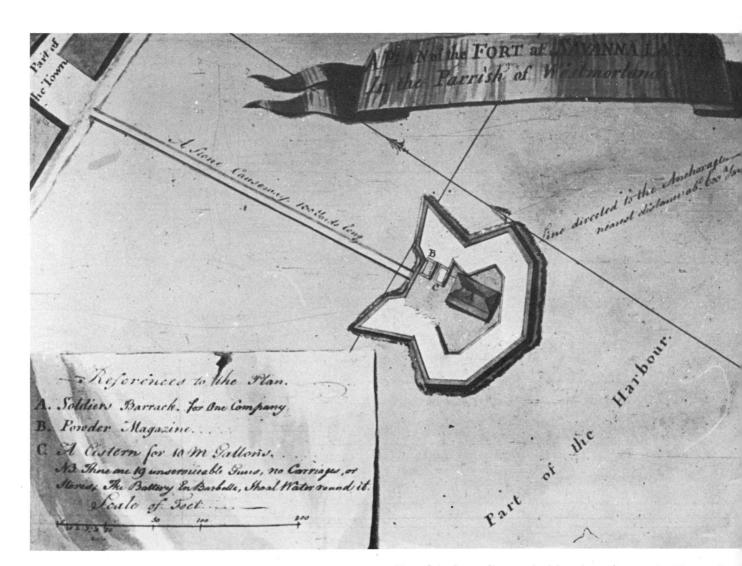

Plan of the fort at Savanna-la-Mar, drawn in 1774 by Thomas Cras...

Aerial view of Savanna-la-M...

Fortifications

The British Period:

Fort George has a remarkable situation, at the end of the promontory which separates the east and the west harbours at Port Antonio. It was begun in 1729, following the plan of Colonel Christian Lilly, whom we have already met as one of the early planners of Kingston (page 12);

today it survives largely intact, and houses Titchfield School. On the plan, the letter 'g' marks 'part of the town of Titchfield'; Port Antonio was formerly known as Titchfield, after the name of one of the Hampshire estates of the first Duke of Portland, governor of Jamaica in 1723 when the town was founded.

As the plan notes, Fort George was designed to be defended by 22 24-pounder guns, and three of these may still be seen in the aerial photograph, standing on original carriages. Also visible in the aerial photograph is a vessel of the U.S. Navy, getting under way from her anchorage in the East Harbour.

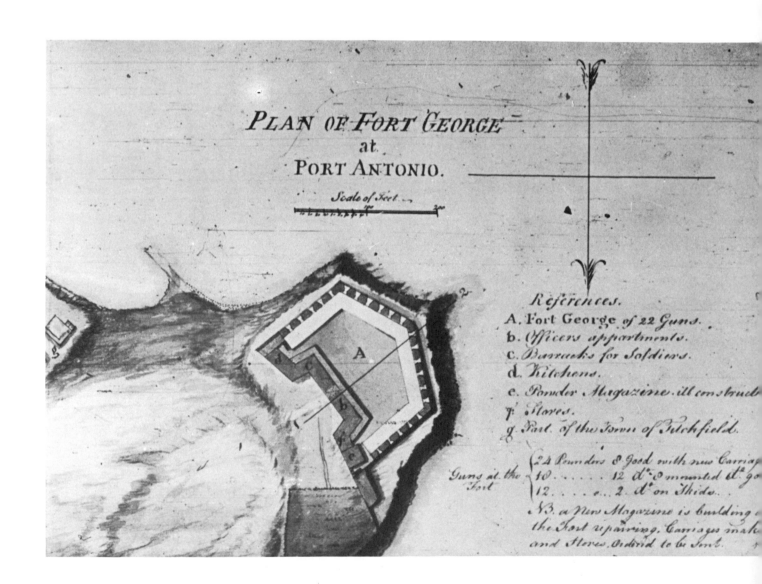

*Plan of the fort at Port Antonio, drawn in 17
by Thomas Craskell*

24

Fortifications

The British Period:

Fort George has a remarkable situation, at the end of the promontory which separates the east and the west harbours at Port Antonio. It was begun in 1729, following the plan of Colonel Christian Lilly, whom we have already met as one of the early planners of Kingston (page 12);

today it survives largely intact, and houses Titchfield School. On the plan, the letter 'g' marks 'part of the town of Titchfield'; Port Antonio was formerly known as Titchfield, after the name of one of the Hampshire estates of the first Duke of Portland, governor of Jamaica in 1723 when the town was founded.

As the plan notes, Fort George was designed to be defended by 22 24-pounder guns, and three of these may still be seen in the aerial photograph, standing on original carriages. Also visible in the aerial photograph is a vessel of the U.S. Navy, getting under way from her anchorage in the East Harbour.

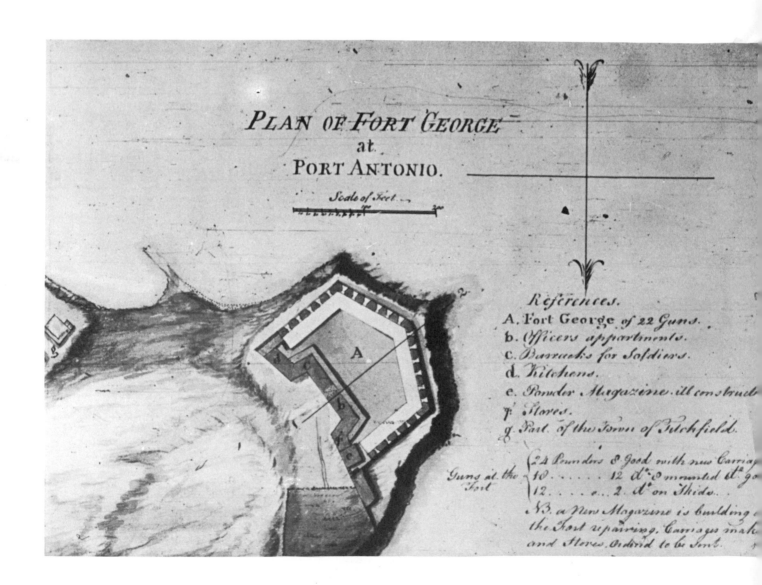

Plan of the fort at Port Antonio, drawn in 17
by Thomas Craskell

Fortifications

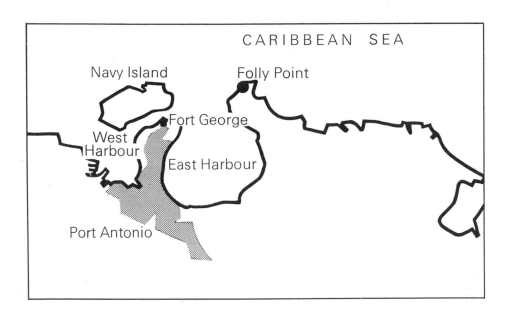

Aerial view of Titchfield School

The British Period:

The old fort at Lucea, like the one at Port Antonio, now houses a secondary school, in this case Rusea's, a foundation dating back to the 1760s. Fort Lucea, as it was at first called, was probably constructed about 1750, and some time after 1760 was named Fort Charlotte in honour of George III's queen.

It is not easy to see the relationship between the plan and the aerial photograph, on which the very site of the circular magazine seems to have disappeared. Howeve[r] as at Port Antonio there are still some guns mounted on their original carriages, and the little fortress is delightfully situated.

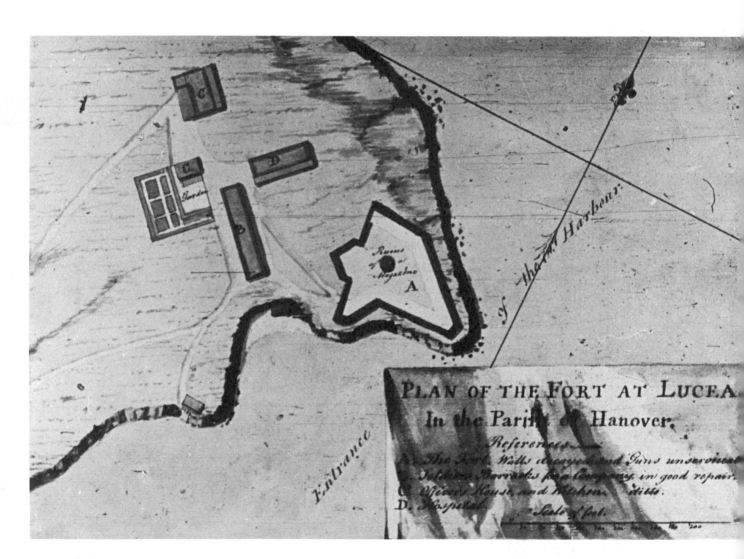

Plan of the fort of Lucea, drawn in 1774 by Thomas Crask

Aerial view of the fort at Lu[cea]

26

Fortifications

The British Period:

In the late 1770s, the military commanders of the Kingston area began to fear that the French might use irregular (Irish) troops to force a way into the Liguanea plain from the mountains to the east of it. One of the river-valleys which seemed to be vulnerable to this kind of assault was the one running north from Bull Bay to Newstead; a fortification —of which nothing survives—was therefore constructed at Drummond's Hill, just south of Newstead.

Drummond's Hill is clearly marked on the plan, and can also be seen on the aerial photograph as the pronounced ridge barring the valley —an excellent site for defensive works. It is in general instructive to compare the plan and the aerial photograph, to appreciate the skill with which the cartographer has drawn this very difficult terrain.

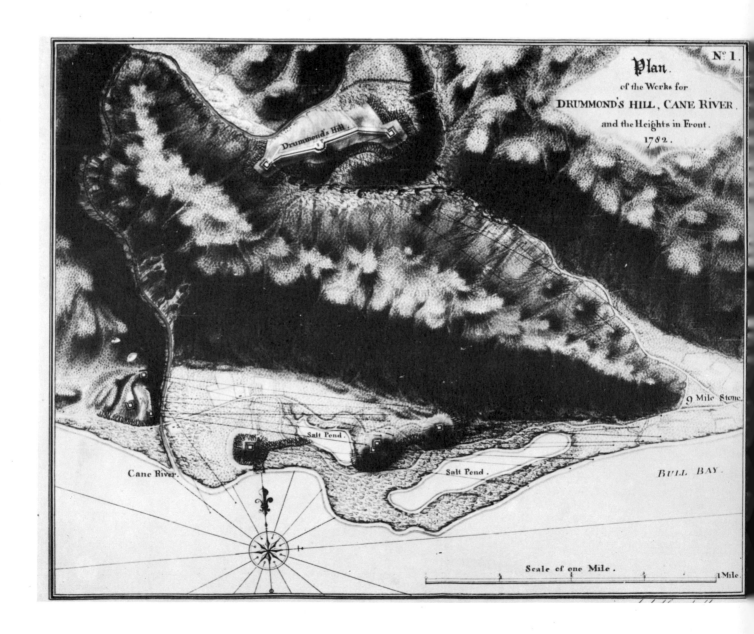

Fortifications

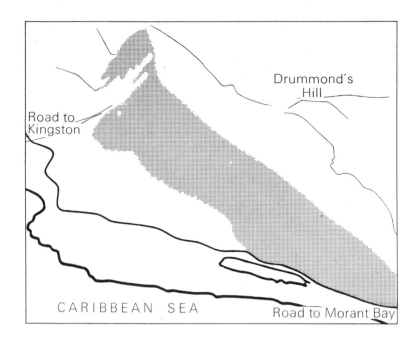

...an of Drummond's Hill and its neighbourhood,
...wn in 1782 by Major-General Campbell

...rial view of the approaches to Drummond's Hill

The British Period:

If the enemy had succeeded in forcing Drummond's Hill (pages 28–29), the next stronghold was to have been at Dallas Castle, on the upper Cane River, which in turn was to have been protected by batteries on Thorn Hill Ridge.

The aerial photograph eloquently reveals the topography of this region, with the ridge running diagonally across the left-hand top corner, and the river winding its way between scrubby banks far below. It is hard to believe that even Irish irregulars would have been capable of forcing a way through this unpromising country.

Fortifications

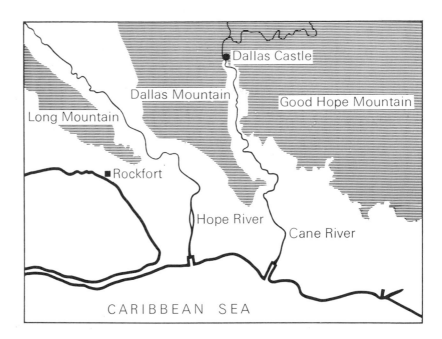

Plan of the Dallas region. Drawn in 1782 by Major-General Campbell

Aerial view of the Dallas Castle area

31

The British Period:

Aerial view of the cantonment at Newcast

Fortifications

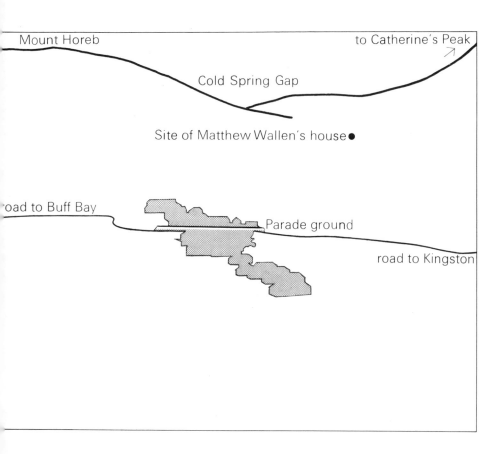

In the mid-eighteenth century there lived just below Cold Spring Gap a certain Matthew Wallen, who seems to have introduced those temperate plants like watercress and wild tansy which are still to be found near the ruins of his house. Wallen died in the 1770s; around 1760 the adjacent hill was scaled by Catherine, sister of the historian Edward Long, who gave her name to Catherine's Peak.

By the early 1840s the once well-tended coffee plantations of these hills had disappeared, with the collapse of the coffee market, and most of the land reverted to bush. It was then that Sir William Gomm, newly-appointed commander-in-chief of the British troops in Jamaica, had the idea of establishing a hill-station at Newcastle, which appeared to be free from yellow fever.

Work was begun in 1841, and the value of the new site was soon apparent. For whereas there were 100 deaths in the first two months out of the 400 members of the newly-arrived King's Royal Rifle Corps stationed down in the plain, none of the 130 soldiers stationed at Newcastle had perished. With the value of the station thus established, similar camps were projected for areas like Trinidad and Hongkong.

Today the Newcastle camp, whose elevation ranges from 3,500 to 4,000 feet, still straggles down the hill below Mount Horeb. It is now the depot of the Jamaica Regiment, but the visitor can still detect certain buildings which look as if they date from the mid-nineteenth century.

The British Period:

The aerial photograph shows an area which will soon be entirely transformed, as it forms part of an intensive development of housing and industry. Just to the south of the Caymanas racecourse (1) may still be seen the old road from Spanish Town to Passage Fort (2). This track has lost its importance, and has been supplanted for through traffic by the modern tarmac road (3). The very site of Passage Fort can now be identified only by digging (4), as the silting of the Rio Cobre (5) has completely altered the line of the coast in the past two hundred years (6, approximate former coastline).

One of the hedgelines is still clearly identifiable (7), as are the fields called Coach-horse (8), Deer Park (9), Old Negroe Ground (10) and Brick-work (11). The former Little Salt Pond Road seems to have been obliterated, but a section of the old track to the south of the salt pond is still visible (12). Away to the east, projecting into Kingston Harbour, the Mosquito Point fort is still easily recognizable (see also pages 18–19); it is the dominating feature of this area, which two hundred years ago supported a thriving estate, but which is at the moment derelict.

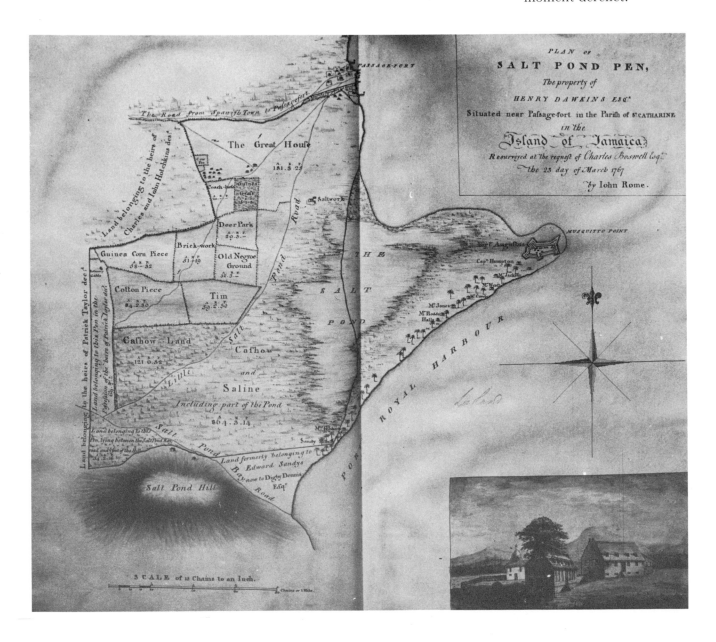

Estates and
Great Houses

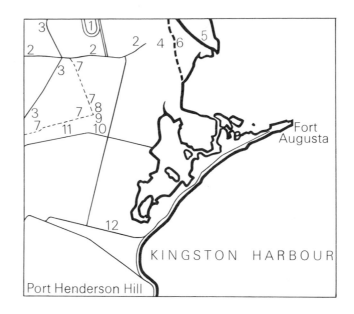

...an of the area between Naggo Head and Passage
...rt, drawn in 1767 by John Rome

...rial view of the area between Naggo Head and
...ssage Fort

The British Period :

Worthy Park, remarkably situated in the secluded Lluidas Vale, was an estate for long associated with the Price family, whose most celebrated member was Sir Charles Price, speaker in the House of Assembly at a crucial juncture between 1756 and 1763. The plan of 1850 is rather disappointing when compared with

the aerial photograph, for although features like the sharp bend in the Rio Cobre allow us to establish the comparison with some precision, yet the field pattern seems to have changed beyond recognition, perhaps because sugar is now grown and harvested in a different way.

The aerial photograph brings out

well the way in which the whole estate is hemmed in by the hills, at whose foot a certain amount of citrus is visible. The old airfield, now a golf course and playing-fields, stands out well, as do the factory itself (see also page 58) and the Rio Cobre, winding its way southwards from its sink-hole in the foothills.

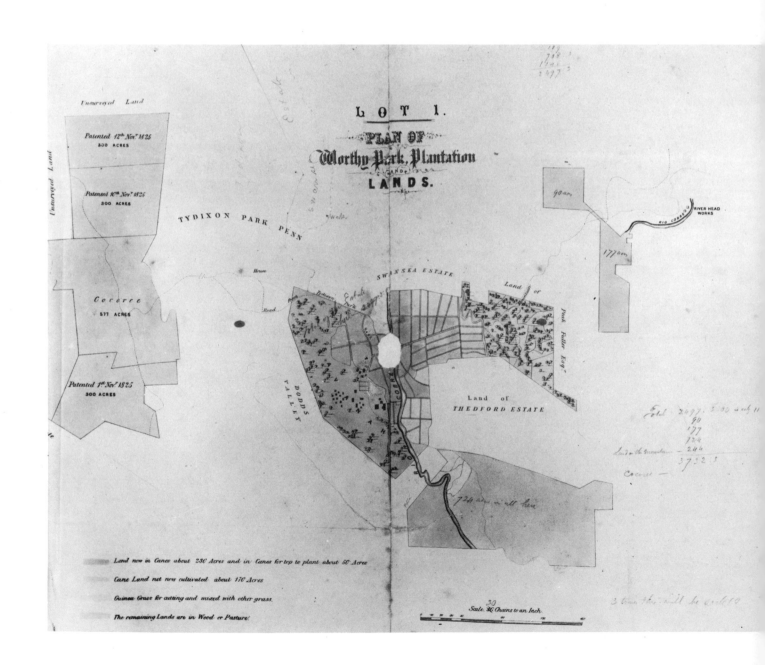

aerial view of the Vale of Lluidas

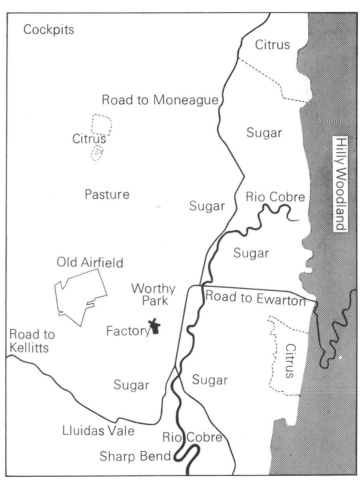

Cockpits

Citrus

Road to Moneague

Citrus

Sugar

Pasture

Sugar

Rio Cobre

Hilly Woodland

Sugar

Old Airfield

Worthy Park

Road to Ewarton

Factory

Road to Kellitts

Citrus

Sugar

Sugar

Lluidas Vale

Rio Cobre

Sharp Bend

Plan of Worthy Park estate, drawn about 1850

The British Period:

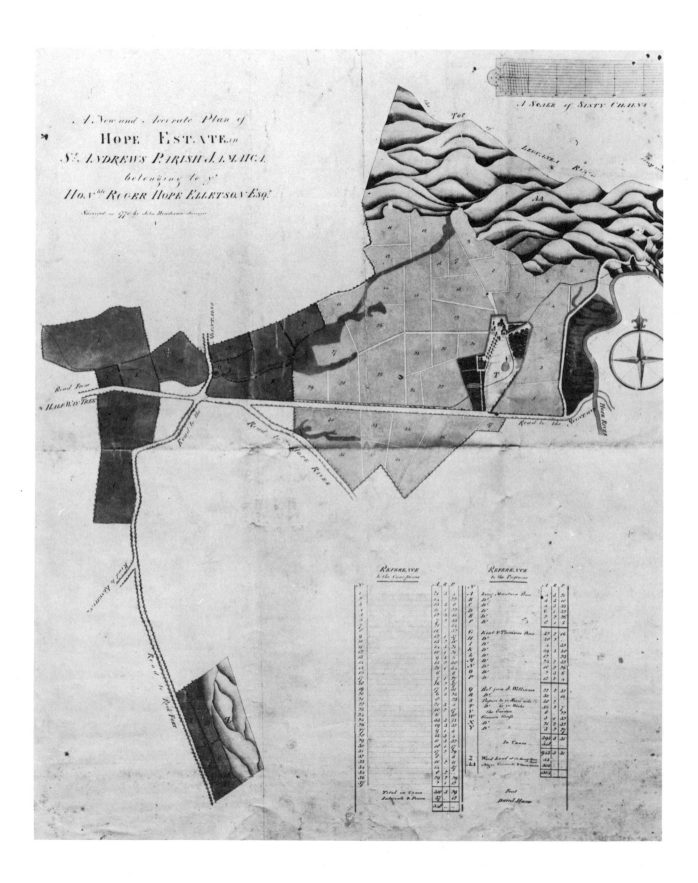

Estates and Great Houses

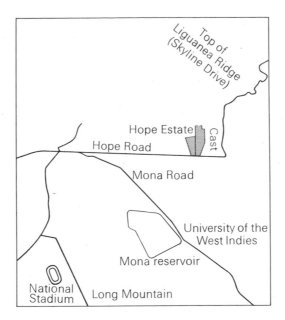

he Hope Estate owes its name to
ajor Richard Hope, one of the
ldiers who came over with
enables from England in 1655.
riting 150 years later, Lady Nugent
scribed it thus: 'As you enter the
tes there is a long range of negro
uses, like thatched cottages, and a
w of cocoa-nut trees and clumps of
tton-trees. The sugar-house, and
the buildings, are thought to be
ore than usually good and well
ken care of'.

The negro houses are clearly
ible on the plan, drawn some 40
ars earlier, as are the aqueduct
hose ruins survive) and the works.
e aerial photograph shows that
central area of the estate
rvives intact, no doubt because
ce 1872 it has formed part of the
pe Royal Botanical Gardens. The
ecision of the early draftsman is
own by his rendering of the
rves in the Hope River; it will be
ticed that the road-pattern has
anged little. The new housing
ates, the National Stadium, the
ona reservoir and the University
the West Indies (see also pages
–71), all stand out well on the
ial photograph.

n of the Hope estate, drawn in 1770 by
n Henderson
ial view of Hope Gardens and the
ounding area

The British Period:

This estate, on the right-hand bank of the Yallahs river at its mouth, was once famous for the sugar known in England as 'white Albion'. Now its aqueduct, works and house are in ruins, and it seems impossible to match the individual fields on the plan with the fields on the aerial photograph. However, the general shape of the estate, lying north and south of the coastal road, is still evident.

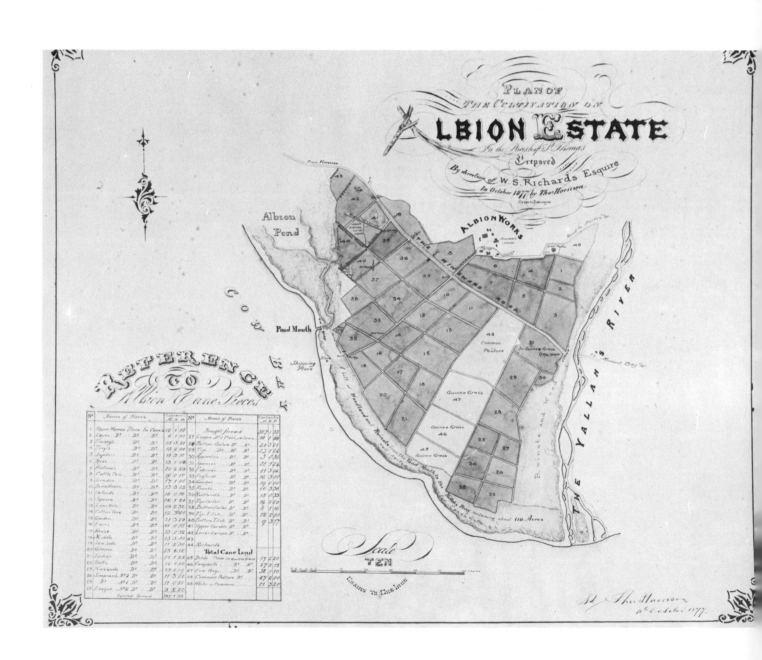

Estates and Great Houses

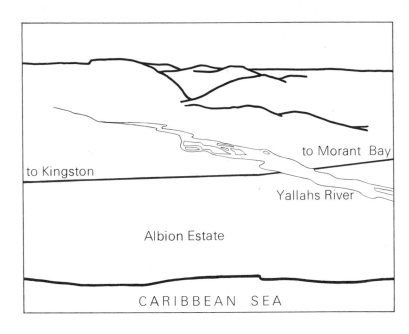

Plan of the Albion Estate, drawn in 1877 by Thomas Harrison

Aerial view of the mouth of the Yallahs river

The British Period:

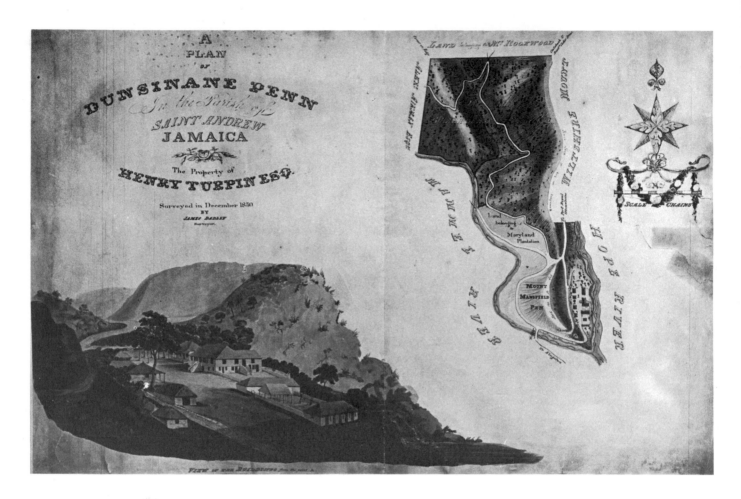

Dunsinane Pen was a small coffee plantation, just across the road from where Blue Mountain Inn now stands. James Dadley's plan gives us a good idea of how it looked in 1830, and the aerial photograph provides a striking example of Jamaican topography, from the house perched on its aerie at the left, down into the river valley, and up again by the steeply-winding Newcastle road.

A private house now stands on the area of the main buildings, but certain fragments of the earlier structure (e.g. the main stairway) still survive in the grounds.

Plan of Dunsinane Pen, drawn in 1830 by James Dadley

Aerial view of the Newcastle road near Blue Mountain Inn

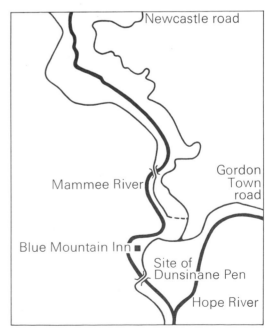

The British Period:

The Bellevue Great House, which stands in delightful grounds a little way off the Mannings Hill road, is persistently associated with Admiral Nelson. However, as is the case with so many Jamaican great houses, it is very difficult to obtain any precise information about its past; evidently it was a coffee and pimento property, and at the height of its prosperity employed about 50 slaves.

A comparison of the plate with the aerial photograph shows that its main lines have not changed very much, though each wing has been somewhat extended. On the aerial photograph, to the left, may be seen the barbecue on which the coffee berries were dried, while on the pla in the centre background, may be seen the Stony Hill barracks, which still stand. Until recently Bellevue was the Catholic diocesan seminary it has now passed into private hand

From Nature & on Stone by J.B. Kidd, R.S.A.

PLATE 40.

BELLE VUE.

RESIDENCE NEAR KINGSTON, STONEY HILL IN THE DISTANCE.

Barwick, 2, Shorter's Court, Throg

Estates and Great Houses

...ngraving of Bellevue by Joseph B. Kidd in 1839–40

...erial view of Bellevue

Mannings Hill

Stony Hill

Bellevue ■

Route A3 to Annotto Bay

Mary Brown's Corner

The British Period:

Estates and Great Houses

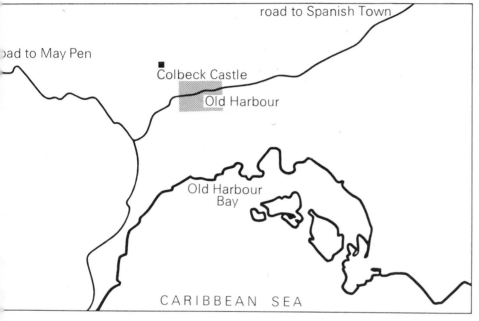

road to Spanish Town

 road to May Pen

Colbeck Castle

Old Harbour

Old Harbour Bay

CARIBBEAN SEA

rial view of Colbeck Castle

Colbeck Castle is a very remarkable structure, which includes a large central building standing within a square enclosure, each side of which is nearly 100 yards long. At the four corners of this enclosure are large outbuildings, linked by a wall which gives the whole complex a fortified appearance.

The aerial photograph shows how impressive the ruins are; it is therefore all the more astounding that it is impossible to say with any precision when the house was constructed. Colonel John Colbeck, after whom it was presumably named, was one of the officers in the English army of the 1655 invasion; he settled in Jamaica and died in 1682. Colbeck Castle certainly looks like the kind of centre at which the militia could rally, and it is sited in a good place for repelling any hostile landing at Old Harbour Bay.

However, if it was in fact constructed in the seventeenth-century as a rallying-point for the militia, it is very curious that we find no mention of it in the writings of the time. It is only fair to add that it does not seem to have been described or sketched at *any* time before 1896, though that does not seem a good reason for ascribing it to the late nineteenth century. Instinct and common-sense would indicate the mid-eighteenth century as the likeliest time, but nothing is less sure . . .

The British Period:

Aerial view of New Forest Great House

Estates and Great Houses

The ruins of New Forest Great House stand about half a mile back from the road between Alligator Pond and Gutters, near the village of the same name. For once, thanks to an article by Ray Fremmer (see bibliography), we know about the construction of this great house, with its superb hall and its magnificent timbers in floor and ceiling.

This was the house of Charles Fulford, who came to Jamaica in 1839, just after emancipation, and at first settled with his parents at Wickwar, near Mount Pleasant in Manchester. Marrying Isabella Dennison, he took over her shop at French Park, just south of Spur Tree, became prosperous and died in 1896. New Forest Great House, also known as Fulford Great House, therefore dates from the latter part of the nineteenth century, and even in its ruined state is worth visiting.

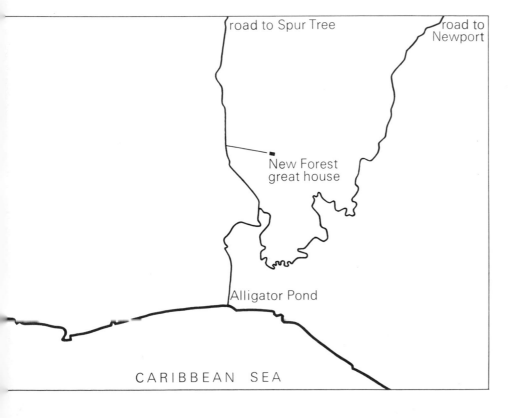

The British Period:

The great house at Rose Hall was built about the middle of the eighteenth century, at the then considerable cost of £30,000. It seems to have been particularly well constructed, for as one account says:

Its floors and stairs, wainscoting and ceiling, doors and windows, were of mahogany, cedar, rosewood, ebony, orange and other native hardwoods of various colours, fit for cabinet-work, highly-polished and well arranged.

This splendid house had by 1960 reached the state of dilapidation shown below; happily it was purchased in 1966 by an owner intent on its restoration, and by 1968 this work had reached the stage shown on the opposite page. It is now open to the public.

Rose Hall is of course famous as the estate of the 'White Witch', who murdered her husbands and flogged her slaves; alas for a picturesque story, there seems, following recent researches, to be little fact behind this fantasy.

Aerial view of Rose Hall in 1960

Estates and
Great Houses

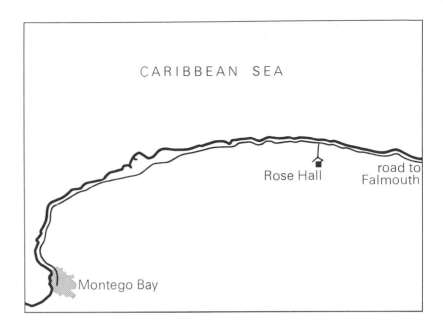

CARIBBEAN SEA

Rose Hall

road to
Falmouth

Montego Bay

...rial view of Rose Hall in 1968

1865 and 1907:

Aerial view of the court-house at Morant Bay

Morant Bay

The aerial photograph shows the court-house at Morant Bay. In 1865 this was the scene of a famous massacre, when the parish council, which included the local magistrate, was attacked by a group of local men, led by Paul Bogle, demanding more equitable administration of justice. The court-house was hastily defended by a company of local volunteers, but the mob forced them back inside the building which was then fired; most of the defenders were cut down as they emerged.

When the news of this insurrection reached Governor Eyre at Flamstead (see page 54) he intensified the preparations which he had already begun, knowing that trouble was brewing; forces were brought round by sea from Port Royal, and from Newcastle by Mahogany Vale. Soon the disorganized rebels were dispersed, and in the ensuing period of martial law more than four hundred people were killed, with or without trial.

This bloody retaliation produced a painful effect on the British government, and a Royal Commission was sent out to investigate the whole affair and to recall Eyre. He was never given any other official position, and several of his colleagues were severely censured. There were also constructive results from the Morant Bay rebellion, as it came to be called; Jamaica's constitution was changed to that of a Crown Colony, which meant that a more efficient administration replaced that of the local ruling class, and the British Government became stricter—in its worldwide network of colonies—in allowing troops to be used for the repression of internal disorders.

Today the court-house has been restored; in front stands the statue of Paul Bogle by Edna Manley, wife of the statesman Norman Manley, and behind may be seen the great cannon which formerly defended the Morant Bay fort.

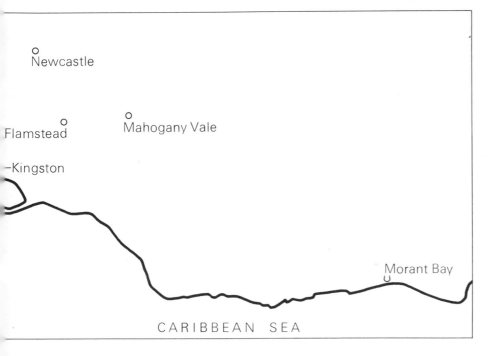

1865 and 1907:

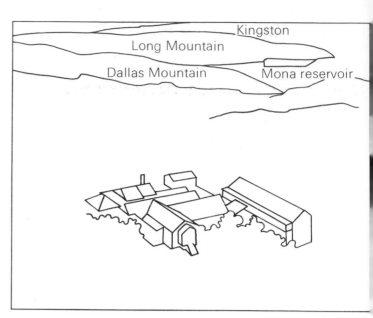

Aerial view of the great house at Flamstead

Flamstead

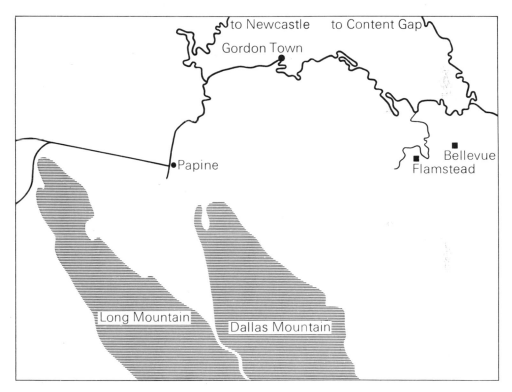

In 1863 Jamaica was visited by Raphael Semmes, captain of the Confederate commerce-raider the *Alabama*. Having been well received in Kingston, Semmes went up to Flamstead, of which he wrote that:

I was in an entirely new world— in those mountains of Jamaica— and was enchanted with everything I saw.

A little later in that year Flamstead was bought by Governor Eyre who, as we have noted, was staying there at the time of the Morant Bay Rebellion. Tradition holds that Nelson, as well as subsequent naval captains, stayed at Flamstead, whence they could communicate with the forts and batteries of the harbour by mirror signals.

The aerial photograph brings out Flamstead's position very well, on a seaward ridge of the Port Royal Mountains. Far below is the Mona Reservoir, by the University of the West Indies, and then beyond Long Mountain may be seen the city and water-front of Kingston. The original great house was destroyed in the earthquake of 1907, but Flamstead has been rebuilt as a guest-house which combines a splendid view with great tranquillity. It is accessible by the same road as the one which leads to Bellevue (see page 56).

1865 and 1907:

The great house at Bellevue is said to have been built about 1793 by a French emigré named Arbouin, who no doubt came from Haiti. After that it passed into the hands of the Strupar family, ancestors of Stonewall Jackson, and from them to Sir Alexander Swettenham, governor of the island between 1904 and 1907. Today it is the mountain-house of the University of the West Indies, where staff and students come to relax and study; it enjoys splendid views not only over the Grand Ridge of the Blue Mountains, seen in the aerial photograph, but also over Kingston harbour.

Sir Alexander Swettenham, who was much concerned with the afforestation of the adjacent countryside, and who received many distinguished visitors at Bellevue, was the governor of Jamaica at the time of the 1907 earthquake, which almost entirely destroyed the city of Kingston. Very soon help arrived, in the shape of three U.S. warships under the command of a certain Admiral Davis. The sailors got quickly to work on shore, but Davi was unfortunately persuaded to lan a party of marines to guard the American consulate. Swettenham took umbrage at this admittedly irregular action, and asked the American admiral to withdraw the marines; Davis in his turn became offended and sailed away with his supplies. The upshot of this sorry affair was that Swettenham apologized to Davis and resigned a governor.

Bellevue and Plumb Point

...rial view of the wreck of the Texita *in 1960*

...rial view of Bellevue

This aerial photograph shows the freighter *Texita*, of Port Arthur, Texas, shortly after she went aground off Plumb Point on 1 September 1960. This view, which also shows the eastern end (29) of the Palisadoes runway, is interesting because it clearly reveals the large wreck on which the *Texita* was impaled, and from which she never freed herself.

Legend has it that this other, larger vessel was a German liner called the *Bremen*, which went aground when the Plumb Point lighthouse was extinguished during the 1907 earthquake; it has, however, been impossible to verify this tale. Another interesting aspect of the photograph is the apparent outline of another large ship, inshore from the presumed *Bremen*; was this yet another victim of treacherous Plumb Point?

Independent Jamaica:

The sugar factory on the Worthy Park Estate

The general layout of this estate has already been illustrated on pages 36–37. To the right and in front of the present buildings may be seen the water-wheel of the former factory, which was powered by water from the aqueduct running in at the left; behind the factory on the right are citrus-orchards and grazing-grounds, while to the left are some fields of cane. Behind rise the redoubtable hills which ring the estate.

Sugar was, of course, the crop on which the great prosperity of eighteenth-century Jamaica was based, but the industry is declining. Intensified competition overseas, coupled with domestic opposition to mechanization and grave labour problems, make it dubious if the Jamaican sugar industry can long survive on its present scale, as the leading agricultural export. Needless to say, any considerable reduction in sugar-production would lead to ever more pressing social problems.

Sugar and Bananas

...tour-planting of bananas in St Mary.

he Jamaican banana industry, in
ntrast to the sugar industry, is
sed primarily on small
asant-holdings rather than on
eat estates. This system of
nd-tenure brings its own problems,
tably in the shape of a product
ich is unpredictable in volume
d often inferior in quality; it is
rd to see how an industry

handling so perishable a product,
destined for distant markets, can
efficiently be run by many small
producers.

The aerial photograph shows an
unusually well-planted area; notice
the rugged terrain and the way in
which dense scrub covers
uncultivated land.

Independent Jamaica:

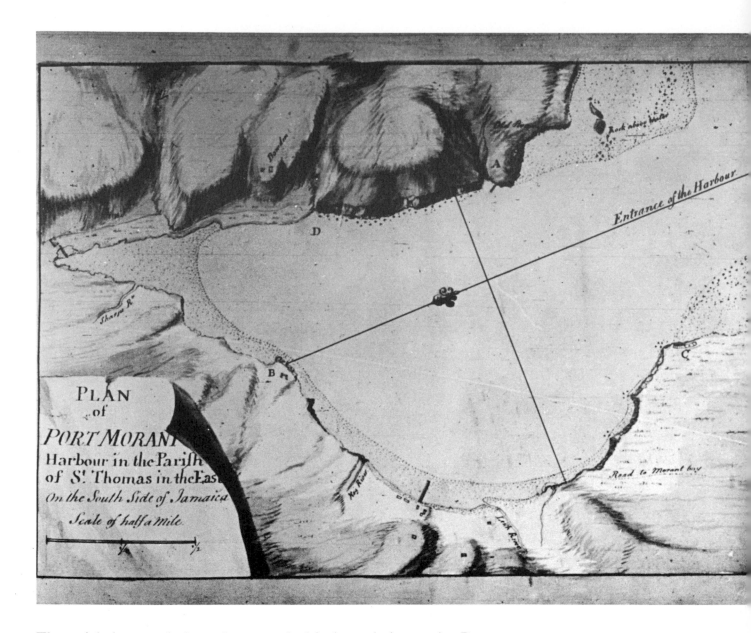

The aerial photograph shows the remarkable harbour at Port Morant, on which the banana-loading wharf of Bowden is situated. Almost all the points mentioned on the eighteenth-century plan are readily identifiable on the photograph. The banana shed is situated about point D on the plan, and the 'rock above water' is clearly visible. Port Morant is the straggling village in the bottom centre of the aerial view; running away to the right is the 'road to Morant Bay'.

A Banana Port

rial view of Port Morant and the banana quay
Bowden

n of Port Morant, drawn by Thomas Craskell
774

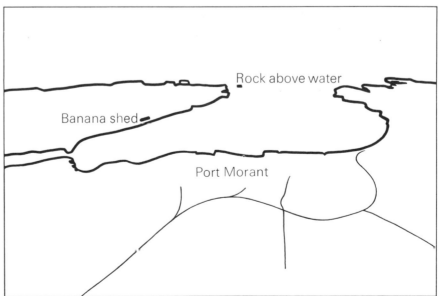

Rock above water

Banana shed

Port Morant

Independent Jamaica:

The gathering of the citrus crop

'Citrus', by which is meant not only oranges and grapefruit but also ortaniques and uglis, ranks third among Jamaica's export crops. It is grown all over the island, but thrives best on the uplands of Clarendon and Manchester. The aerial photograph shows grapefruit being loaded in bulk into lorries probably for local processing; the choicest fruit is normally boxed for overseas markets.

Citrus and Tobacco

Tobacco fields and drying houses near May Pen

The tobacco crop does not play a significant part in Jamaica's agricultural exports, but tourists learn to appreciate the virtues of the Jamaican cigar, strong-flavoured yet smooth and relatively cheap. The plate shows tobacco fields and drying houses near May Pen, in Clarendon.

Independent Jamaica:

Bauxite: the Alcan alumina plant at Ewarton

It was in 1943 that the first cargo of Jamaican bauxite was exported, to be tested for its aluminium content by Alcan of Canada. The tests having shown that Jamaican bauxite, despite a high iron content, was suitable for the production of aluminium, mines were established not only by Alcan but also by Reynolds, Kaiser and Alcoa. By the late 1960s bauxite and alumina accounted for about half the total value of Jamaican exports, and had thus come to play a vital part in the island's economy; indeed, Jamaica then produced nearly a quarter of all the bauxite mined in the world.

Bauxite and Tourism

Tourism: the Tower Isle Hotel

The tourist industry has since the Second World War seen a spectacular boom along Jamaica's splendid north coast, and this development shows little sign of slowing down. Thanks largely to skilful work by the Jamaican Tourist Board in its North American offices, visitors have recently been coming to the island at the rate of over 300,000 new arrivals each year.

The effect of a large tourist industry on any country's economic and social structure is of course hard to assess. In Jamaica many of the largest hotels are foreign-owned, which often means that a large part of the profits does not stay in the island. In social terms, it is plainly disquieting when ostentatiously luxurious hotels are constructed alongside the cramped hovels in which too many Jamaicans still have to live.

Independent Jamaica:

Aerial view of the port of Kingston

Commerce

most the whole of Jamaica's
neral overseas commerce now
mes through the port of Kingston,
here the old wharves (see also
ge 12) had begun to prove quite
adequate for its greatly increased
lume. A new harbour was
erefore created at Newport West,
here a whole commercial and

industrial complex is expected to
develop; this will be complemented
by the wharves at Newport East.

Just to the west of this site,
too, a causeway is in course of
construction across Hunts Bay; when
this is completed and opened to
motor traffic, a whole new area,
formerly desolate marsh (see page

35), will be opened for housing and
industrial development. Kingston,
hemmed in to the north and to the
east by the mountains, will thus
be able to expand towards the
west, eventually no doubt beyond
Port Henderson and across the
Hellshire Hills.

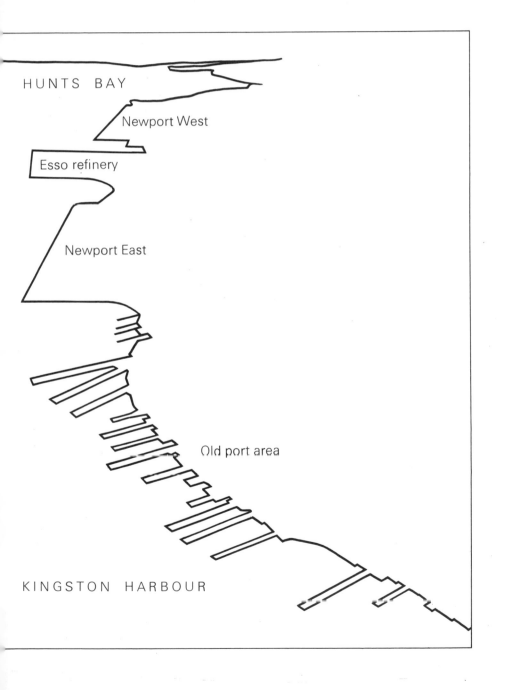

HUNTS BAY

Newport West

Esso refinery

Newport East

Old port area

KINGSTON HARBOUR

Independent Jamaica:

Aerial view of part of West Kingston

Housing Conditions

...ial view of Beverly Hills

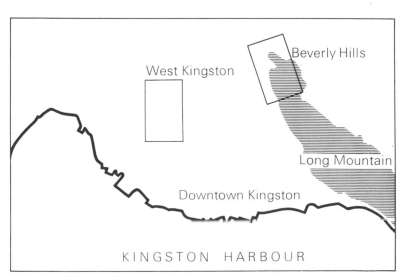

...me sociologists like to speak of 'the
...o Jamaicas', and this pair of
...rial photographs is a good
...stration of what they mean. On
...e left is a view of part of West
...ngston, and above a view of
...e new houses at Beverly Hills,
... the Long Mountain overlooking
...ngston. The contrast is too
...king to require commentary.

Independent Jamaica:

These two plates show the site of the University of the West Indies, first in 1955 and then in 1968. In every part of the two photographs the contrast is striking, not only in the area of the University, but also to the south (top) and west (right) of it; a housing estate has emerged where there was formerly a mango-grove, the Mona reservoir has been completed (see also pages 38–39),

and the National Stadium has been constructed.

The University is a multi-national institution, supported by most of the English-speaking territories of the Caribbean area; it has not only the Mona campus, but others on Trinidad and Barbados, as well as extra-mural centres on many of the smaller islands. It naturally suffers from occasional bouts of chauvinism

on the part of certain contributory governments, but on the whole succeeds in its task of providing a focal point of higher learning in a region which desperately needs cultural and technical institutions all kinds. Started in 1948 with abo 30 students, the University by 1968 had about 3,000 students, and was due for continued expansion.

Aerial view of the University College of the West Indies in 1955

Higher Education

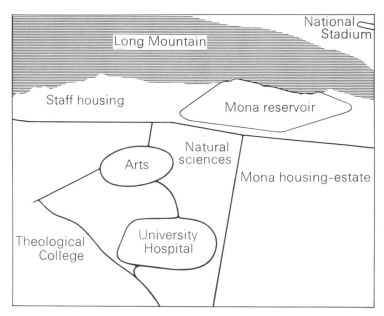

Long Mountain

National Stadium

Staff housing

Mona reservoir

Arts

Natural sciences

Mona housing-estate

Theological College

University Hospital

rial view of UWI in 1968

Independent Jamaica:

The arrival of HMS Britannia *in 1966*

The photograph above shows HMS *Britannia* rounding the point of Port Royal in March 1966, when the Queen and Prince Philip came on an official visit to Jamaica. On the opposite page is seen the *United States* manoeuvring into the dock at Newport West, with the town of Kingston and the Blue Mountains in the background.

These two final photographs are perhaps symbolic of a steady change in the pattern of Jamaica's foreign relations. Whereas until 1962 she looked instinctively to Great Britain for advice and support, after independence her relations with North America tended to become increasingly close. With the continuing decline of sugar and bananas, traditional exports to Great Britain, and the growing importance of the bauxite and tourist industries, both of which are North-American orientated, it seems certain that this tendency will become even more marked in the future.

External Relations

e United States *about to dock at Newport West*

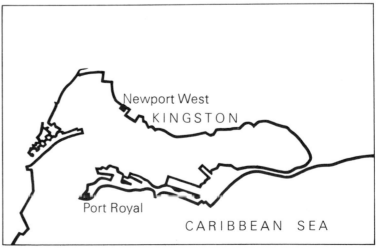